W9-CDX-923

Velociraptor

by Wil Mara

Content Consultant
Gregory M. Erickson, PhD
Paleontologist
The Florida State University
Tallahassee, Florida

Reading Consultant
Jeanne Clidas
Reading Specialist

Children's Press®
An Imprint of Scholastic Inc.
New York Toronto London Auckland Sydney
Mexico City New Delhi Hong Kong
Danbury, Connecticut

Library of Congress Cataloging-in-Publication Data
Mara, Wil.
  Velociraptor/by Wil Mara.
    p. cm.—(Rookie read-about dinosaurs)
  Includes bibliographical references and index.
  ISBN-13: 978-0-531-20864-9 (lib. bdg.)   ISBN-10: 0-531-20864-8 (lib. bdg.)
  ISBN-13: 978-0-531-20933-2 (pbk.)   ISBN-10: 0-531-20933-4 (pbk.)
  1. Velociraptor—Juvenile literature. I. Title. II. Series.
  QE862.S3M3336 2012
  567.912—dc23   2011032712

SCHOLASTIC, CHILDREN'S PRESS, ROOKIE READ-ABOUT®, and associated
logos are trademarks and/or registered trademarks of Scholastic Inc.

1 2 3 4 5 6 7 8 9 10   R 21 20 19 18 17 16 15 14 13 12

Photographs © 2012: Alamy Images/Jim Zuckerman: cover, 12; Black Hills Institute
of Geological Research, Inc./Timothy Larson: 28, 29; Getty Images/Highlights for
Children: 16, 17, 31 bottom left; Photo Researchers/Chris Butler: 8, 9, 31 top right;
Shutterstock, Inc./Ralf Juergen Kraft: 14, 15, 18, 19, 31 bottom right; Superstock,
Inc./Stocktrek Images: 20; The Image Works/The Natural History Museum:
4, 6, 22, 23, 24, 26, 31 top left.

TABLE OF CONTENTS

MEET THE VELOCIRAPTOR

The Velociraptor (vuh-LAHS-ih-rap-tur) was a small dinosaur.

It had feathers all over its body.
The feathers kept it warm.

Its arms looked like wings.
But it could not fly.

It walked on its two back legs.

SMALL IS GOOD

The Velociraptor was around 6 feet (2 meters) long from head to tail. It was about as heavy as a collie dog. It was as long as a couch.

The Velociraptor had a long neck. The neck could bend and stretch.

14

Its head was also very long.

BUILT FOR SPEED

The Velociraptor ran very fast. It had strong back legs.

18

It also held its tail out.
The tail helped it make
turns when moving fast.

DINNERTIME

The Velociraptor ate other animals. It did not eat plants.

22

It also ate animals that had already died.

A FIERCE HUNTER

The Velociraptor was a
fierce hunter. It had very
sharp teeth to bite its prey.

26

The Velociraptor's front claws were long and sharp. It used its claws to kill prey.

DINOSAUR BONES

Scientists found Velociraptor bones. They built a skeleton from the bones. It is in a museum.

Can you find the toes on each foot on this skeleton? Can you find the tail?

TRY THIS! Go back in the book to page 9 with your child. Ask her if she can find the three claws on each front foot in the illustration. Then ask her how the Velociraptor used the claws (to catch prey). Compare other parts of the skeleton such as the sharp teeth and the long neck with this illustration to review what your child read in the book.

The name Velociraptor means "speedy thief."

One Velociraptor fossil was found with the bones of another dinosaur. They died fighting each other.

Visit this Scholastic web site for more information on the Velociraptor: **www.factsfornow.scholastic.com**

WORDS YOU KNOW

claw

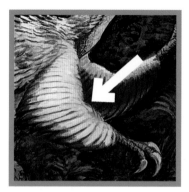

feathers

tail

Velociraptor

Index

Learn More!

You can learn more about the Velociraptor at:

www.bbc.co.uk/nature/life/Velociraptor

About the Author

Wil Mara is the award-winning author of more than 100 books, many of them educational titles for young readers. More information about his work can be found at *www.wilmara.com*.